THE DEEPER LIFE

THE DEEPER LIFE

GOING BEYOND KNOWLEDGE
TO EXPERIENCE
SPIRIT-FILLED LIVING

A. W. Tozer

MOODY PUBLISHERS

CHICAGO

Edited by Kevin Mungons
Interior and cover design: Erik M. Peterson
Cover image of liquid blue texture copyright © 2022 by korkeng/Shutterstock (1802211250). All rights reserved.

ISBN: 978-0-8024-2933-9

Originally delivered by fleets of horse-drawn wagons, the affordable paperbacks from D. L. Moody's publishing house resourced the church and served everyday people. Now, after more than 125 years of publishing and ministry, Moody Publishers' mission remains the same—even if our delivery systems have changed a bit. For more information on other books (and resources) created from a biblical perspective, go to www.moodypublishers.com or write to:

Moody Publishers
820 N. LaSalle Boulevard
Chicago, IL 60610

1 3 5 7 9 10 8 6 4 2

Printed in the United States of America

CONTENTS

Introduction

TOZER'S SEARCH FOR A DEEPER LIFE

A. W. Tozer pursued God with unusual zeal, searching for an intimate relationship that he could not fully describe with words. At various times he called it "the deeper Christian life," "deep things of God," or just the "deeper life." But what, exactly, was it? And how do you find it?

His answer came from unlikely places. Not from a conventional education—he skipped high school to work in a rubber factory. And not from seminary training, which he also lacked. His spiritual understanding didn't come from the glut of programs, Bible conferences, or Christian celebrities that rose to popularity in his era. In fact, he found these distracting. He complained that the church culture was producing Bible knowledge without penetrating the heart.

Tozer stripped away the distractions and found an elemental solution based on the power of the Word and the power of the Spirit. He applied these to a close study of Philippians 3:10, where the apostle Paul drew readers into his lifelong passion: "That I may know him, and the power of his resurrection, and the fellowship of his sufferings, being made conformable unto his death."

As Tozer continued to study, he discovered that others had taken the same path before him—the ancient writers, long forgotten, who knew God with an intense personal fervor. Critics called them Christian mystics, and looked darkly at their theological roots. Tozer, however, read with discernment, filtering out the moments of doctrinal confusion and concentrating on matters of the heart.

One book in particular gave Tozer the insights he craved. Written anonymously in the fourteenth century, *The Cloud of Unknowing* asked readers to move past mere knowledge and intellect *about* God. Instead, God should be known—experienced—through intense contemplation, leading the worshiper to feelings of deep love. Tozer immediately recognized the importance of this idea and recognized how it would tweak conventional thought on spiritual growth. For some of the theological gatekeepers, words like *experience* and *feelings* could bring the discussion into tenuous territory.

Another insight came from the book's obsolete word choices, especially its persistent use of the verb *list*—as in, *an earnest and active desire.* Tozer took this as a marching order. Contrary to some contemporary advice ("let go and let God"), the path toward spiritual maturity must be actively pursued. Or, as *Unknowing* put it, "more devoutly and more listily in soberness and in purity and in deepness of spirit."

Oh, the irony! A preacher with an eighth-grade education found spiritual wisdom by reading obscure books written in Middle English. And now that he had discovered these new friends, Tozer wanted to introduce them to his working-class congregation in Chicago (where, it goes without saying, no one read Middle English in their spare time). Tozer's task quickly shifted from one of self-discovery to a much broader responsibility—teaching timeless truths in ways that anyone could understand.

He distilled the essence of his ancient sources into a book that became an instant classic, *The Pursuit of God* (1948). Suddenly his church was crowded with visitors and his mailbox was jammed with speaking invitations. Tozer feared the worst—was he becoming a Christian *celebrity*? Not if he could help it! Bombarded with more projects than he could ever accept, he made careful plans. He reserved his expanded platform for a narrowly defined purpose, devoted to teaching the essence of spiritual renewal to the regular folks in his church.

Others noticed the effectiveness of his approach—including pastors and Christian leaders from surprisingly diverse theological perspectives. Tozer's Reformed friends didn't see eye to eye with him on the mechanics and timing of Spirit filling. And to be sure, Tozer embraced *crisis sanctification*, though he generally avoided using the term. Nevertheless, Tozer asked readers to consider the consequences of their own beliefs. "Perhaps your doctrinal bias is away from belief in the crisis of the Spirit's filling," he says in chapter 8. "Very well, look at the fruit of such doctrine. What is your life producing?"

In retrospect, Tozer's output was astounding. After *The Pursuit of God*, he wrote and preached about the deeper life so many times that the contemporary reader finds it difficult to sort out his essential teaching. As stewards of this literary legacy, Moody Publishers is committed to producing definitive Tozer editions on his best-known themes. *The Deeper Life* marks the first publication of several long-lost articles written for *Moody Monthly* magazine in 1950, curated with other articles from *Christian Life* and *Alliance Witness*. This book marks the first time all this teaching is available in one volume.

Behind the scenes, we've preserved Tozer's text just as he wrote it, with very minimal changes to spelling, punctuation, and mechanics. Perhaps a disclaimer (warning?) might be appropriate here. Despite his passion for connecting to the common person, Tozer did not talk down to anyone, nor did he explain his references to Shakespeare, old hymn texts, and obscure theological treatises. Nowadays, a quick internet search might fill in a few gaps for the curious.

For readers who are just embarking on this search for a deeper spiritual life, welcome! Read *The Pursuit of God* (1948) for devotional meditations with Bible reading and prayer; read *A Deeper Life* (2022) for how-to essays on the basic principles of spiritual maturity; and read *A More Perfect Faith* (2023) for homiletical sermons from Philippians 3. Taken together, these three volumes offer an enormous body of insight on a misunderstood topic. All three books will prod the reader to move beyond a superficial approach to Christian living. For people feeling burned out, experiencing a spiritual vacuum, or missing something in their spiritual lives—congratulations for taking the first step. In *The Pursuit of God*, Tozer expressed gratitude for this new sense of spiritual hunger: "They will not be satisfied till they have drunk deep at the Fountain of Living Water."

—KEVIN MUNGONS, editor

GOD, UNTO WHOM ALL HEARTS BE OPEN,

AND UNTO WHOM ALL WILL SPEAKETH,

AND UNTO WHOM NO PRIVY THING IS HID—

I BESEECH THEE SO FOR TO CLEANSE

THE INTENT OF MINE HEART

WITH THE UNSPEAKABLE GIFT OF THY GRACE,

THAT I MAY PERFECTLY LOVE THEE,

AND WORTHILY PRAISE THEE.

AMEN.

—*THE CLOUD OF UNKNOWING,*
14TH CENTURY

1

ARE WE MISSING SOMETHING?

Many Christians go through life without reflecting on their closeness to God—but when they do, and they find themselves wanting more, be careful! This rewarding path may take you into difficult territory.

It is my serious conviction that there lies within the framework of fundamental Christianity a place of power and fruitfulness far richer and more beautiful than anything the average Christian at present enjoys.

I have arrived at this conviction by a number of converging roads. Starting from any of several points and traveling straight along, I have come out at the same place, namely, that there is in the simple message of the cross something wonderfully elevated and heavenly which has escaped this present generation of

Christians—or at least it has escaped the rank and file of those who make up the great army of conservative believers today.

For one thing—and this is by far the most important—the Bible itself would appear definitely to indicate this. Peter justified the experience of the disciples at Pentecost by saying simply, "This is that." The *that* to which he referred was the promise of God in the Old Testament; the *this* was the sudden afflatus of power which those disciples had received a few minutes before. The two corresponded exactly.

If "this" had not sprung out of "that," Peter and the rest of those Scripture-honoring Jews would have rejected it flatly. But for us the important thing is that the ancient promise *did* come alive in human experience; it *did* leave its place on the Hebrew scroll and enter the living hearts of believing men and women. That which had for hundreds of years been a sacred and well-guarded text now leaps into life and becomes a wondrous, conscious reality in the souls of living men.

We have but to take a quick look at our "this," which is our present experiential possession, and compare it with "that," which is what God tells us we could possess if we would, and the startling spiritual discrepancy is instantly apparent.

Another road that led me to the conclusion that we of this day are missing something very wonderful in the Christian life is the road of religious biography. Making every allowance for the spirit of hero worship and the naïve enthusiasm with which religious biographers often approach the task of writing the lives of the saints, I could not escape the conviction that such men as Augustine, Bernard of Clairvaux, Johannes Tauler, and Nicholas of Cusa (to mention but a few of the ancients) *must* have had a knowledge of

God leagues beyond anything we see in conservative circles today.

As a seeker after God I found it rather disquieting to compare the spiritual fervor of such men as François Fénelon, Jonathan Edwards, Samuel Rutherford, or John Wesley with our casual and rather self-satisfied twentieth-century fundamentalism.

Another thing that disturbed me was the fact that the saints of whom I speak were not what they were because of any superior intellectual gifts (though many of them possessed intellects of the first order). Their power lay in their intimate knowledge of God. The aura that picks them out of the shadows of the past was something from God, something spiritual, something inward and heavenly. And when I learned that they had found their treasure within the sacred Scriptures and could give chapter and verse for all they enjoyed, I knew that I at least was missing something which I might possess if I would.

> **THE WEAKEST BELIEVER HOLDS IN HIS HAND ALL THAT THE MIGHTIEST SAINTS EVER POSSESSED.**

Here is an odd fact: the weakest believer holds in his hand all that the mightiest saints ever possessed. He has at his disposal every grace that made them what they were. This weakest believer actually believes the same things that made an Augustine, a Nicholas Herman, or a Samuel Rutherford. The difference is not one of creed, but of emphasis and experience.

One more road I might mention that brought me to the conclusion that we of today are missing untold spiritual treasures was my own personal experience of God. Through much suffering and with many slips and falls I have been (through infinite grace) led into a land where the grass is longer and the waters cooler than any

I have known before. And all this without altering one tenet of my fundamentalist creed, and without admitting anything as genuine which cannot be justified by the Scriptures of truth.

Knowing that some good people might call me a mystic or an extremist, and having on my own account a rather cautious mind, I have carefully checked everything as it occurred by the two tests of Scripture and fruit, and I have come to this conclusion: whatever leads a man to adore the Triune God and to trust with growing appreciation the precious blood of atonement; whatever makes him hate sin more intensely, love the brethren with broader charity, love the Word of God as the very fountain of all truth, love God's ancient people, the Jew; respect and obey the laws of the land, and work for the evangelization of the lost world—whatever, I say, has this effect cannot be false or fanatical. It must be of God.

HINDERANCES TO A DEEPER SPIRITUAL LIFE

Now, nothing comes causeless. The thin, bloodless quality of much that claims to be Christian, the failure of believers to enter into their heritage in Christ, the habit of dragging on year after year without spiritual power, the tendency to "grovel here below, fond of these earthly toys," and the general absence of that moral happiness and spiritual delight which characterized the first Christians, must have a cause.

We dare not say that cause is wrong doctrine, for these things are true of multitudes who believe in the whole Bible and who have never deviated an iota from the truth as taught by the apostles. They are true of many in Bible schools and in missionary societies, and they are true of many sincere ministers of Christ and leaders of the conservative forces of our day. To what then do we trace our failure? What prevents the seed of truth from springing into flower and fruit?

Without pretending to solve the whole problem in a few words, I would nevertheless point out some hindrances which should be plain enough to everyone once the brush is cleared away.

A loss of subjective faith. One thing is this, that for more than a full generation we have been under the influence of a type of Christian teaching which (intentionally or not) constantly stressed the objectivity of the Christian faith at the expense of its subjectivity. Stated simply, the objective in religion is that which is external to me, the subjective is that which is within me. Whatever the psychologists might think of this definition, it yet does define the words as I shall use them.

Now the two elements must be kept in balance if we are to have the true faith of the New Testament. But this we have not done. In our praiseworthy effort to preserve correct doctrine and to magnify the finished work of Christ, we have unconsciously created the impression that Christianity is an objective thing, consisting of certain acts of God done outside of us and apart from us in time and place. We have stressed objective truth to the near exclusion of subjective experience. We have led people to believe that if they accept the historic truth of Christianity, they do indeed possess its true spiritual content.

I submit that the historic facts of Christianity do not constitute the faith of our Fathers. They constitute instead only one-half of it. The other half consists of the contemporary acts of God done within the souls of men, based upon and springing out of the historic acts already accomplished.

A lack of inner zeal. This almost exclusive preoccupation with the objective elements in the Christian religion has created a generation of textualists characterized by a burning zeal for the letter of the faith, but at the same time revealing a strange lack of understanding of its subjective and experiential elements. Everything is in the text, but the textualists do not explain how to get the vital content of the text into our hearts. The interiority of true faith is overlooked, and we find ourselves like a hungry boy counting the bread and rolls through the thick plate glass of the bakery window. If the boy were to compose a song about what he sees, or write a book telling the number, size, and shape of the loaves in the window, he might win himself a reputation as a pretty good fundamentalist.

I am afraid that for a long time we have been doing just that. We stand greatly in need of men to tell us how to get the bread through the plate glass and into our famished bodies.

There is a justly famous German work (too little known in our day) called *Theologia Germanica.* This little book had a powerful effect upon the life and ministry of Martin Luther, and he was himself responsible for several editions being printed and circulated. The author is unknown, but whoever he was, he saw the pitfall which textualism digs for the feet of unwary Christians, and wrote against it with great clarity and vigor. We would do well to heed his words:

> We should mark and know of a very truth that all manner
> of virtue and goodness, and even that Eternal Good which
> is God Himself, can never make a man virtuous, good or

happy, so long as it is outside the soul. . . . In like manner all the great works and wonders that God has ever wrought or shall ever work in or through the creatures, or even God Himself with all His goodness, so far as these things exist or are done outside of me, can never make me blessed, but only insofar as they exist and are done and loved, known, tasted, and felt within me.

A loss of basic morality. Another cause of spiritual debility in evangelical circles is the divorce between faith and moral living. Without meaning to do it, we have left the impression that there is an impassable gulf between faith and life. And the great emphasis has been upon faith, so that countless thousands have accepted Christ as Savior (if such a thing is possible) without any corresponding shift of attitude toward the world or the flesh.

To teach or believe that true faith divorced from practice is possible to a human being is to convict ourselves of ignorance of both psychology and theology. All things being equal, *a man is what he believes*, and any faith which is not accompanied by a radical moral change is instantly disqualified and proved to be no true faith at all.

A shallow understanding of the gospel. One more hindrance to the deeper life which I would mention is undue emphasis upon the *escape element* in the gospel. To a sinner trembling on the brink of the abyss, there could hardly be sweeter words than those found in John 3:16, "shall not perish." They are hope in despair, they are light in a dungeon, and they are reprieve and escape from the house of death.

Because this is so, and the dramatic moment lies right there,

ANY FAITH WHICH IS NOT ACCOMPANIED BY A RADICAL MORAL CHANGE IS INSTANTLY DISQUALIFIED AND PROVED TO BE NO TRUE FAITH AT ALL.

the preacher is likely to make much of it and to present it over and over again, returning to it night after night, supporting it with touching stories and pointing everything up to the happy moment when the reprieve is granted. The escape element is so glorious that it tends to become the beginning and the end of many persons' experience.

Bible teachers too often gear back their exposition to this event and make no provisions for anything beyond it. And if the beginner is urged to "go on," the exhortation usually means little more than that he should study to learn all the reprieve means to him and to marshal more Scripture dealing with that happy truth. The psychology of spiritual advance is destroyed at its start.

I think it can hardly be denied that this describes vast numbers of believers in circles of unimpeachable orthodoxy. These poor sheep simply have no one to show them, either by precept or example, what a glorious world of spiritual riches they entered when the reprieve was granted. So they build little houses on the very borders of the land and never explore the sweet uplands that beckon them on. They then settle down to lives marked by disappointment (which is met by gritting their teeth and exercising "faith"), dull monotony, and pensive hope of something better when the Lord returns.

Now I believe there is for all of us a better life than that. There is a place of power, of inner sweetness, of personal communion with the Triune God, of victory over self, of swift flights on eagle's wings, of moral delights and spiritual fullness which we all may enjoy. I shall be eternally grateful to our Lord if He sees fit through these chapters to stimulate even a very few to seek such a place for themselves.

BEFORE YOU START: A WARNING

If God has singled you out to be a special object of His grace, you may expect Him to honor you with stricter discipline and greater suffering than less favored ones are called upon to endure.

And right here let me anticipate the objection someone is sure to raise, viz., that God has no "specials" among His children. The Holy Scriptures and Christian history agree to show that He has. Star differs from star in glory among the saints on earth as well as among the glorified in heaven. Without question the differences exist; but whether they are by the decree of God or by His foreknowledge of the degree of receptivity He will find among His children I am not prepared to say with certainty, though I would lean strongly to the latter view.

If God sets out to make you an unusual Christian, He is not likely to be as gentle as He is usually pictured by the popular teachers. A sculptor does not use a manicure set to reduce the rude, unshapely marble to a thing of beauty. The saw, the hammer and the chisel are cruel tools, but without them the rough stone must remain forever formless and unbeautiful.

To do His supreme work of grace within you He will take from your heart everything you love most. Everything you trust in will go from you. Piles of ashes will lie where your most precious treasures used to be.

21

This is not to teach the sanctifying power of poverty. If to be poor made man holy, every vagrant on a park bench would be a saint. But God knows the secret of removing things from our hearts while they still remain to us. What He does is to restrain us from enjoying them. He lets us have them but makes us psychologically unable to let our hearts go out to them. Thus they are useful without being harmful.

All this God will accomplish at the expense of the common pleasures that have up to that time supported your life and made it zestful. Now under the careful treatment of the Holy Spirit your life may become dry, tasteless, and to some degree a burden to you.

While in this state you will exist by a kind of blind will to live; you will find none of the inward sweetness you had enjoyed before. The smile of God will be for the time withdrawn, or at least hidden from your eyes. Then you will learn what faith is; you will find out the hard way, but the only way open to you, that true faith lies in the will, that the joy unspeakable of which the apostle speaks is not itself faith but a slow-ripening fruit of faith; and you will learn that present spiritual joys may come and go as they will without altering your spiritual status or in any way affecting your position as a true child of the heavenly Father. And you will also learn, probably to your astonishment, that it is possible to live in all good conscience before God and men and still feel nothing of the "peace and joy" you hear talked about so much by immature Christians.

How long you continue in this night of the soul will depend upon a number of factors, some of which you may be able later to identify, while others will remain with God, completely hidden from you. The words "The day is thine, the night is also thine" will now be interpreted for you by the best of all teachers, the Holy Spirit; and you will know by personal experience what a blessed thing is the ministry of the night.

But there is a limit to man's ability to live without joy. Even Christ could endure the cross only because of the joy set before Him. The strongest steel breaks if kept too long under unrelieved tension. God knows exactly how much pressure each one of us can take. He knows how long we can endure the night, so He gives the soul relief, first by welcome glimpses of the morning star and then by the fuller light that harbingers the morning.

Slowly you will discover God's love in your suffering. Your heart will begin to approve the whole thing. You will learn from yourself what all the schools in the world could not teach you—the healing action of faith without supporting pleasure. You will feel and understand the ministry of the night: its power to purify, to detach, to humble, to destroy the fear of death and, what is more important to you at the moment, the fear of life. And you will learn that sometimes pain can do what even joy cannot, such as exposing the vanity of earth's trifles and filling your heart with longing for the peace of heaven.

GOD KNOWS EXACTLY HOW MUCH PRESSURE EACH ONE OF US CAN TAKE. HE KNOWS HOW LONG WE CAN ENDURE THE NIGHT.

What I write here is in no way original. This has been discovered anew by each generation of Christian seekers and is almost a cliche of the deeper life. Yet it needs to be said to this generation of believers often and with emphasis, for the type of Christianity now in vogue does not include anything as serious and as difficult as this. The quest of the modern Christian is likely to be for peace of mind and spiritual joy, with a good degree of material prosperity thrown in as an external proof of the divine favor.

Some will understand this, however, even if the number is relatively small, and they will constitute the hard core of practicing saints so badly needed at this serious hour if New Testament Christianity is to survive to the next generation.

2

NO REVIVAL WITHOUT REFORMATION

*Our commitment to Bible doctrine seems admirable—
but mere intellectual knowledge is ineffective without
the power of the Holy Spirit. True spiritual reformation
starts with personal cleansing.*

Wherever Christians meet these days, one word is sure to be heard constantly repeated; that word is *revival*.

In sermon, song, and prayer we are forever reminding the Lord and each other that what we must have to solve our spiritual problems is a "mighty, old-time revival." The religious press, too, has largely gone over to the proposition that revival is the one great need of the hour, and anyone who is capable of preparing a brief for revival is sure to find many editors who will publish it.

So strongly is the breeze blowing for revival that scarcely anyone appears to have the discernment or the courage to turn around and lean into the wind, even though the truth may easily lie in that direction. Religion has its vogues—as do philosophy, politics, and women's fashions. Historically, the major world religions have had their periods of decline and recovery, and those recoveries are bluntly called revivals by the annalists.

Let us not forget that in some lands Islam is now enjoying a revival, and the latest report from Japan indicates that after a brief eclipse following World War II, Shintoism is making a remarkable comeback. In our own country Roman Catholicism, as well as liberal Protestantism, is moving forward at such a rate that the word *revival* is almost necessary to describe the phenomenon. And this without any perceptible elevation of the moral standards of its devotees.

A religion, even popular Christianity, could enjoy a boom altogether divorced from the transforming power of the Holy Spirit and so leave the church of the next generation worse off than it would have been if the boom had never occurred. I believe that the imperative need of the day is not simply revival, but a radical reformation that will go to the root of our moral and spiritual maladies and deal with causes rather than with consequences, with the disease rather than with symptoms.

It is my considered opinion that under the present circumstances we do not want revival at all. A widespread revival of the kind of Christianity we know today in America might prove to be a moral tragedy from which we would not recover in a hundred years.

Here are my reasons. A generation ago, as a reaction from

higher criticism and its offspring, modernism, there arose in Protestantism a powerful movement in defense of the historic Christian faith. This, for obvious reasons, came to be known as fundamentalism. It was a more or less spontaneous movement without much organization, but its purpose wherever it appeared was the same: to stay the rising tide of negation in Christian theology and to restate and defend the basic doctrines of New Testament Christianity. This much is history.

> **I BELIEVE THAT THE IMPERATIVE NEED OF THE DAY IS NOT SIMPLY REVIVAL, BUT A RADICAL REFORMATION THAT WILL GO TO THE ROOT OF OUR MORAL AND SPIRITUAL MALADIES.**

FALLING VICTIM TO ITS VIRTUES

What is generally overlooked is that fundamentalism, as it spread throughout the various denominations and nondenominational groups, fell victim to its own virtues. The Word died in the hands of its friends. Verbal inspiration, for instance (a doctrine which I have always held and do now hold), soon became afflicted with *rigor mortis*. The voice of the prophet was silenced, and the scribe captured the minds of the faithful. In large areas the religious imagination withered. An unofficial hierarchy decided what Christians were to believe. Not the Scriptures, but what the scribe thought the Scriptures meant became the Christian creed. Christian colleges, seminaries, Bible institutes, Bible conferences, popular Bible expositors all joined to promote the cult of textualism. The system of extreme dispensationalism—

which was devised—relieved the Christian of repentance, obedience, and cross-carrying in any other than the most formal
sense. Whole sections of the New Testament were taken from
the church and disposed of after a rigid system of "dividing the
Word of truth."

All this resulted in a religious mentality inimical to the true
faith of Christ. A kind of cold mist settled over fundamentalism.
Below, the terrain was familiar. This was New Testament Christianity, to be sure. The basic doctrines of the Bible were there, but
the climate was just not favorable to the sweet fruits of the Spirit.

The whole mood was different from that of the early church
and of the great souls who suffered and sang and worshiped in
the centuries past. The doctrines were sound but something vital
was missing. The tree of correct doctrine was never allowed to
blossom. The voice of the turtle dove was rarely heard in the
land; instead, the parrot sat on his artificial perch and dutifully
repeated what he had been taught, and the whole emotional tone
was somber and dull. Faith, a mighty, vitalizing doctrine in the
mouths of the apostles, became in the mouth of the scribe another
thing altogether and power went from it. As the letter triumphed,
the Spirit withdrew and textualism ruled supreme. It was the time
of the believer's Babylonian captivity.

In the interest of accuracy it should be said that this was a
general condition only. Certainly there were some even in those
low times whose longing hearts were better theologians than
their teachers were. These pressed on to a fullness and power
unknown to the rest. But they were not many and the odds were
too great; they could not dispel the mist that hung over the land.

The error of textualism is not doctrinal. It is far more subtle than that and much more difficult to discover, but its effects are just as deadly. Its theological beliefs are not at fault—but its assumptions are.

It assumes, for instance, that if we have the word for a thing, we have the thing itself. If it is in the Bible, it is in us. If we have the doctrine, we have the experience. If something was true of Paul it is of necessity true of us because we accept Paul's epistles as divinely inspired. The Bible tells us how to be saved, but *textualism goes on to make it tell us that we are saved*, something which in the very nature of things it cannot do. Assurance of individual salvation is thus no more than a logical conclusion drawn from doctrinal premises, and the resultant experience wholly mental.

REVOLT FROM MENTAL TYRANNY

Then came the revolt. The human mind can endure textualism just so long before it seeks a way of escape. So, quietly and quite unaware that any revolt was taking place, the masses of fundamentalism reacted, not from the teaching of the Bible but from the mental tyranny of the scribes. With the recklessness of drowning men they fought their way up for air and struck out blindly for greater freedom of thought and for the emotional satisfaction their natures demanded and their teachers denied them.

The result over the last twenty years has been a religious debauch hardly equaled since Israel worshiped the golden calf. Of us Bible Christians it may truthfully be said that we "sat down to eat and to drink, and rose up to play." The separating line between the church and the world has been all but obliterated.

Aside from a few of the grosser sins, the sins of the unregenerated world are now approved by a shocking number of professedly "born-again" Christians, and copied eagerly. Young Christians take as their models the rankest kind of worldlings and try to be as much like them as possible. Religious leaders have adopted the techniques of the advertisers; boasting, baiting, and shameless exaggerating are now carried on as a normal procedure in church work. The moral climate is not that of the New Testament, but that of Hollywood and Broadway.

THE SEPARATING LINE BETWEEN THE CHURCH AND THE WORLD HAS BEEN ALL BUT OBLITERATED.

Most evangelicals no longer initiate; they imitate, and the world is their model. The holy faith of our fathers has in many places been made a form of entertainment, and the appalling thing is that all this has been fed down to the masses from the top.

That note of protest which began with the New Testament and which was always heard loudest when the church was most powerful has been successfully silenced. The radical element in testimony and life that once made Christians hated by the world is missing from present-day evangelicalism. Christians were once revolutionists—moral, not political—but we have lost our revolutionary character. It is no longer either dangerous or costly to be a Christian. Grace has become not free, but cheap. We are busy these days proving to the world that they can have all the benefits of the gospel without any inconvenience to their customary way of life. It's "all this, and heaven too."

This description of modern Christianity, while not universally applicable, is yet true of an overwhelming majority of present-day Christians. For this reason it is useless for large companies of believers to spend long hours begging God to send revival. Unless we intend to reform we may as well not pray. Unless praying people have the insight and faith to amend their whole way of life to conform to the New Testament pattern there can be no true revival.

UNLESS PRAYING PEOPLE HAVE THE INSIGHT AND FAITH TO AMEND THEIR WHOLE WAY OF LIFE TO CONFORM TO THE NEW TESTAMENT PATTERN THERE CAN BE NO TRUE REVIVAL.

WHEN PRAYING IS WRONG

Sometimes praying is not only useless, it is wrong. Here is an example: Israel had been defeated at Ai, and "Joshua rent his clothes, and fell to the earth upon his face before the ark of the LORD until the eventide, he and the elders of Israel, and put dust upon their heads" (Josh. 7:6).

According to our modern philosophy of revival, this was the thing to do and, if continued long enough, should certainly have persuaded God and brought the blessing. But "the LORD said unto Joshua, Get thee up; wherefore, liest thou upon thy face? Israel hath sinned, and they have also transgressed my covenant which I commanded them. . . . Up, sanctify the people, and say, Sanctify yourselves against to morrow: for thus saith the LORD God of Israel, There is an accursed thing in the midst of thee, O Israel: thou canst not stand before thine enemies, until ye take away the accursed thing from among you" (Josh. 7:10–13).

We must have a reformation within the church. To beg for a flood of blessing to come upon a backslidden and disobedient church is to waste time and effort. A new wave of religious interest will do no more than add numbers to churches that have no intention to own the lordship of Jesus and come under obedience to His commandments. God is not interested in increased church attendance unless those who attend amend their ways and begin to live holy lives.

Once the Lord through the mouth of the prophet Isaiah said a word that should settle this thing forever:

> To what purpose is the multitude of your sacrifices unto me? saith the LORD: I am full of the burnt offerings of rams, and the fat of fed beasts; and I delight not in the blood of bullocks, or of lambs, or of he goats. When ye come to appear before me, who hath required this at your hand, to tread my courts? Bring no more vain oblations; incense is an abomination unto me; the new moons and sabbaths, the calling of assemblies, I cannot away with; it is iniquity, even the solemn meeting. . . . Wash you, make you clean; put away the evil of your doings from before mine eyes; cease to do evil; learn to do well; seek judgment, relieve the oppressed, judge the fatherless, plead for the widow. . . . If ye be willing and obedient, ye shall eat the good of the land. (Isa. 1:11–17, 19)

Prayer for revival will prevail when it is accompanied by radical amendment of life; not before. All-night prayer meetings that are not preceded by practical repentance may actually be displeasing to God. "To obey is better than sacrifice" (1 Sam. 15:22).

We must return to New Testament Christianity, not in creed only but in complete manner of life as well. Separation, obedience, humility, simplicity, gravity, self-control, modesty, cross-bearing: these all must again be made a living part of the total Christian concept and be carried out in everyday conduct. We must cleanse the temple of the hucksters and the money changers and come fully under the authority of our risen Lord once more. And this applies to this writer and to these books as well as to everyone that names the name of Jesus. Then we can pray with confidence and expect true revival to follow.

3

THE DEEPER LIFE: WHAT IT IS

With five simple words the apostle Paul starts us on the path of new understanding: "That I may know Him." This fresh yearning for deeper spiritual riches is transforming the church, one heart at a time.

Suppose some angelic being who had since creation known the deep, still rapture of dwelling in the divine Presence would appear on earth and live awhile among us Christians. Don't you imagine he might be astonished at what he saw?

The angel might, for instance, wonder how we can be contented with our poor, commonplace level of spiritual experience. In our hands, after all, is a message from God not only inviting us into His holy fellowship but also giving us detailed instructions about how to get there. After feasting on the bliss of intimate communion with God, how could such a being understand the casual, easily satisfied spirit which characterizes most evangelicals today? And if our hypothetical angel knew such blazing souls as Moses, David, Isaiah, Paul, John, Stephen, Augustine, Rolle, Rutherford, Newton, Brainerd, and Faber, he might logically conclude that twentieth-century Christians had misunderstood some vital doctrine of the faith somewhere and had stopped short of a true acquaintance with God.

What if an angel sat in on the daily sessions of an average Bible conference and noted the extravagant claims we Christians make for ourselves as believers in Christ and compared them with our actual spiritual experiences? He would surely conclude that there was a serious contradiction between what we think we are and what we are in reality. The bold claims that we are sons of God, that we are risen with Christ and seated with Him in heavenly places, that we are indwelt by the life-giving Spirit, that we are members of the body of Christ and children of the new creation, are negated by our attitudes, our behavior and, most of all, by our lack of fervor, and by the absence of a spirit of worship within us.

Perhaps if our heavenly visitor pointed out the great disparity between our doctrinal beliefs and our lives, he might be dismissed with a smiling explanation that it is but the normal difference between our sure standing and our variable state. Certainly then, he would be appalled that as beings once made in the image of God we could allow ourselves thus to play with words and trifle with our own souls.

Significant, isn't it, that of all who hold the evangelical position, those Christians who lay the greatest store by Paul are often the least Pauline in spirit. There is a vast and important difference between a Pauline creed and a Pauline life. Some of us who have for years sympathetically observed the Christian scene feel constrained to paraphrase the words of the dying queen and cry out, "O Paul! Paul! What evils have been committed in thy name." Tens of thousands of believers who pride themselves on their understanding of Romans and Ephesians cannot conceal the sharp spiritual contradiction that exists between their hearts and the heart of Paul.

> **THOSE CHRISTIANS WHO LAY THE GREATEST STORE BY PAUL ARE OFTEN THE LEAST PAULINE IN SPIRIT.**

That difference may be stated this way: Paul was a seeker and a finder and a seeker still. They seek and find and seek no more. After "accepting" Christ they tend to substitute logic for life and doctrine for experience.

For them the truth becomes a veil to hide the face of God; for Paul it was a door into His very Presence. Paul's spirit was that of the loving explorer. He was a prospector among the hills of God searching for the gold of personal spiritual acquaintance. Many today stand by Paul's doctrine who will not follow him in his passionate yearning for divine reality. Can these be said to be Pauline in any but the most nominal sense?

IF PAUL WERE PREACHING TODAY

With the words "that I may know him," Paul answered the whining claims of the flesh and raced on toward perfection (Phil. 3:10). Paul counted all gain as loss for the excellency of the knowledge of Christ Jesus the Lord, and if to know Him better meant suffering or even death it was all one to Paul. To him conformity to Christ was cheap at any price. He panted after God as the hart pants after the water brook, and calm reason had little to do with the way he felt.

Indeed a score of cautious and ignoble excuses might have been advanced to slow him down, and we have heard them all. "Watch out for your health," a prudent friend warns. "There is danger that you become mentally unbalanced," says another. "You'll get a reputation for being an extremist," cries a third, and a sober Bible teacher with more theology than thirst hurries to assure him that there is nothing more to seek. "You are accepted in the beloved," he says, "and blessed with all spiritual blessings in heavenly places in Christ. What more do you want? You have only to believe and to wait for the day of His triumph."

So Paul would be exhorted if he lived among us today, for so in substance have I heard the holy aspirations of the saints damped down and smothered as they leaped up to meet God in an increasing degree of intimacy. But knowing Paul as we do, it is safe to assume that he would ignore this low counsel of expediency and press onward toward the mark for the prize of the high calling of God in Christ Jesus. And we do well to follow him.

When the apostle cries, "That I may know him," he uses the word *know* not in its intellectual but in its experiential sense. We must look for the meaning—not to the mind but to the heart. Theological knowledge is knowledge about God. While this is indispensable, it is not sufficient. It bears the same relation to man's spiritual need as a well does to the need of his physical body. It is not the rock-lined pit for which the dusty traveler longs, but the sweet, cool water that flows up from it. It is not intellectual knowledge about God that quenches man's ancient heart-thirst, but the very Person and Presence of God Himself. These come to us through Christian doctrine, but they are more than doctrine. Christian truth is designed to lead us to God, not to serve as a substitute for God.

A NEW YEARNING AMONG CHRISTIANS

Within the hearts of a growing number of evangelicals in recent days has arisen a new yearning after an above-average spiritual experience. Yet most Christians still shy away from it and raise objections that evidence misunderstanding, or fear, or plain unbelief. They point to the neurotic, the psychotic, the pseudo-Christian cultist, and the intemperate fanatic—and lump them all together without discrimination as followers of the "deeper life."

While this is of course completely preposterous, the fact that such confusion exists obliges those who advocate the Spirit-filled life to define their terms and explain their position. Just what, then, do we mean? And what are we advocating?

For myself, I am reverently concerned that I teach nothing but Christ crucified. For me to accept a teaching or even an emphasis, I must be persuaded that it is scriptural and altogether apostolic in spirit and temper. And it must be in full harmony with the best in the historic church and in the tradition marked by the finest devotional works, the sweetest and most radiant hymnody, and the loftiest experiences revealed in Christian biography.

It must lie within the pattern of truth that gave us such saintly souls as Bernard of Clairvaux, John of the Cross, Molinas, Nicholas of Cusa, John Fletcher, David Brainerd, Reginald Heber,

Evan Roberts, General Booth, and a host of other like souls who, while they were less gifted and lesser known, constitute what Dr. Paul S. Rees (in another context) calls "the seed of survival." And his term is apt, for it was such extraordinary Christians as these who saved Christianity from collapsing under the sheer weight of the spiritual mediocrity it was compelled to carry.

To speak of the "deeper life" is not to speak of anything deeper than simple New Testament religion. Rather it is to insist that believers explore the depths of the Christian evangel for those riches it surely contains but which are as surely missing. The "deeper life" is deeper only because the average Christian life is tragically shallow.

They who advocate the deeper life today might compare unfavorably with almost any of the Christians that surrounded Paul or Peter in early times. While they may not as yet have made much progress, their faces are toward the light and they are beckoning us on. It is hard to see how we can justify our refusal to heed their call.

THE "DEEPER LIFE" IS DEEPER ONLY BECAUSE THE AVERAGE CHRISTIAN LIFE IS TRAGICALLY SHALLOW.

What the deeper life advocates are telling us is that we should press on to enjoy in personal inward experience the exalted privileges that are ours in Christ Jesus; that we should insist upon tasting the sweetness of internal worship in spirit as well as in truth; that to reach this ideal we should if necessary push beyond our contented brethren and bring upon ourselves whatever opposition may follow as a result.

The author of the celebrated devotional work *The Cloud of*

Unknowing begins his little book with a prayer that expresses the spirit of the deeper life teaching:

> God, unto whom all hearts be open . . . and unto whom no secret thing is hid, I beseech Thee so for to cleanse the intent of mine heart with the unspeakable of Thy grace; that I may perfectly love Thee and worthily praise Thee. *Amen.*

Who that is truly born of the Spirit, unless he has been prejudiced by wrong teaching, can object to such a thorough cleansing of the heart as will enable him perfectly to love God and worthily to praise Him? Yet this is exactly what we mean when we speak about the "deeper life" experience. Only we mean that it should be literally fulfilled within the heart, not merely accepted by the head. Nicephorus, a father of the Eastern Church, in a little treatise on the Spirit-filled life, begins with a call that sounds strange to us only because we have been for so long accustomed to following Jesus afar off and to living among a people that follow Him afar off.

> You, who desire to capture the wondrous divine illumination of our Savior Jesus Christ—who seek to feel the divine fire in your heart—who strive to sense and experience the feeling of reconciliation with God—who, in order to unearth the treasure buried in the field of your heart and to gain possession of it, have renounced everything worldly—who desire the candles of your souls to burn brightly even now, and who for this purpose have renounced nil the world—who wish by conscious experience to know and to

receive the kingdom of heaven existing within you—come and I will impart to you the science of eternal heavenly life.

Such quotations as these might easily be multiplied till they filled half a dozen volumes. This yearning after God has never completely died in any generation. Always there were some who scorned the low paths and insisted upon walking the high road of spiritual perfection. Yet, strangely enough, that word *perfection* never meant a spiritual terminal point nor a state of purity that made watchfulness and prayer unnecessary. Exactly the opposite was true.

HEARING BUT NOT OBEYING

It has been the unanimous testimony of the greatest Christian souls that the nearer they drew to God, the more acute became their consciousness of sin and their sense of personal unworthiness. The purest souls never knew how pure they were, and the greatest saints never guessed that they were great. The very thought that they were good or great would have been rejected by them as a temptation of the devil.

They were so engrossed with gazing upon the face of God that they took scarce a moment looking at themselves. They were suspended in that sweet paradox of spiritual awareness where they *knew* that they were clean through the blood of the Lamb and yet *felt* that they deserved only death and hell as their just reward. This feeling is strong in the writings of Paul and is found also in almost all devotional books and among the greatest and most-loved hymns.

The quality of evangelical Christianity must be greatly improved if the present unusual interest in religion is not to leave the church worse off than she was before the phenomenon emerged. If we listen I believe we will hear the Lord say to us what He once said to Joshua, "Arise, go over this Jordan, thou, and all this people, unto the land which I do give to them, even to the children of Israel" (Josh. 1:2). Or we will hear the writer to the Hebrews say, "Therefore leaving the principles of the doctrine of Christ, let us go on unto perfection" (Heb. 6:1). And surely we will hear Paul exhort us to "be filled with the Spirit" (Eph. 5:18).

THE PUREST SOULS NEVER KNEW HOW PURE THEY WERE, AND THE GREATEST SAINTS NEVER GUESSED THAT THEY WERE GREAT.

If we are alert enough to hear God's voice, we must not content ourselves with merely "believing" it. How can any man believe a command? Commands are to be obeyed, and until we have obeyed them we have done exactly nothing at all about them. And to have heard them and not obey them is infinitely worse than never to have heard them at all, especially in the light of Christ's soon return and the judgment to come.

4

THE DEEPER LIFE: WHAT IT IS NOT

Many people talk about a "deeper life" without understanding its true meaning. Full consecration comes when we learn to distinguish truth from error. Watch for these five misconceptions.

If we are to find a deeper Christian life, we must also recognize the misconceptions that some have suggested. By the words *deeper life* I do not mean a life deeper than Scripture indicates. I do not want anything that cannot be found within the framework of the Christian revelation. I do not want anything that is added. That is why I never buy books or listen to lectures on how to wake up your solar plexus and tune in to the cosmic processes. All that is extra scriptural—any of it that is good was first taught in the Word of God. So I let those authors write to people who don't know the Word, and I stay by the Word.

I am a Bible Christian, and if an archangel with a wingspread as broad as a constellation shining like the sun were to come and offer me some new truth, I'd ask him for a reference. If the angel could not show me where it is found in the Bible, I would bow him out and say, "I'm awfully sorry, you don't bring any references with you." So what I'm talking about is not a life deeper than the Scriptures indicate, but merely one that is, in fact, what it professes to be in name.

A Christian is not one who has been baptized, necessarily, though a Christian is likely to be baptized. A Christian is not one who receives communion, though a Christian may receive communion, and if he's been properly taught, he will. But that is not a Christian necessarily. A Christian is not one who has been born into a Christian home, though the chances are more likely that he will be a Christian if he has a good Christian background. A Christian is not one who has memorized the New Testament, or is a great lover of Christian music, or who goes to hear the Apollo Club sing the *Messiah* every year. A Christian may do all of those things and I think it might be fine if he did, but that doesn't make one a Christian. A Christian is one who sustains a right relationship to Jesus Christ.

Christians enjoy a kind of union with Jesus Christ. The relationship we sustain may be one of adoring faith and love; it may be one of admiration; it may be one of hostility; it may be one of complete carelessness; but it is an attitude of some sort. Now, a relationship of some sort exists between every human being and Jesus Christ; that is, every human being that ever heard of Jesus Christ. But a

Christian is one who sustains a right and proper relation, a biblical relation, to Jesus Christ. Several contrasts could be made.

THE DEEPER LIFE IS NOT A MOVEMENT

Today there exists within the framework of orthodox Christianity a minority group, constituting a movement or school of religious thought, which is distinguished for its emphasis upon the "deeper life," by which is meant complete consecration to God on the part of the individual, resulting in the filling with the Spirit and a life of victory over sin. Its adherents also stress the potency of prayer as a means of accomplishing things otherwise impossible.

This movement is usually called "Full Gospel," and though we dislike to place any modifiers before the word *gospel*, we let the term stand to identify it off from that which is merely *fundamental*.

Knowing well the shortcomings of the movement, and how it is often embarrassed by the self-imposed friendships of persons of feeble intellect and ill-disciplined emotions, the writer yet declares himself in hearty sympathy with its yearning after a satisfying Christian experience and its belief in the "old-time power." With eyes open we choose to go along with the hungry brother who actually believes that Christ is "the same yesterday, today, and forever," rather than to hang back with the timid half-believer who is more concerned with correct doctrine than with spiritual power.

Without endorsing everything which may be taught in the name of the Full Gospel movement, we yet firmly believe that its emphasis is the scriptural one, that its motion is in the right direction, that its mistakes are the mistakes of faith rather than of unbelief.

THE DEEPER LIFE IS NOT WEAK

And there is no use to deny that we have made and are making our mistakes. Some of these are minor and may be passed over as inconsequential, but others are serious and are costing us heavily. One of these has to do with consecration and the volitional attitude in the surrendered life. A misunderstanding here has slowed us down till it is only by courtesy that we can be called a *movement*—we are not moving in a way that is perceptible to the naked eye. It has, in the name of Christ, tended to discourage initiative and destroy leadership in the work of Christ, as well as to silence the voice of prophetic authority at a time when the church needs it so badly.

It seems our teaching on consecration contains elements of error. In an effort to bring men and women to a place of death to self, we too often break their spines and leave them will-less and dead to all progressive spiritual activity. It appears that we do not know what humility is nor how it operates in life. Our humility is mostly smirking and self-conscious. We confuse it with lamb-like harmlessness and insist upon being sheep always and under all circumstances forgetting that only one aspect of the Christian character is contemplated in that figure of speech. The believer is called a farmer, a soldier, a boxer, and many other things which indicate he is to be a man of burning courage and boundless activity. True humility may be militant; its very weakness may be its strength. The meek man may need not hide away to nurse his weakness; he may rush out like David to slay a giant or win a battle for the Lord.

THE DEEPER LIFE IS NOT AN INFERIORITY COMPLEX

Our trouble is that we have disenfranchised the flesh without learning to get along with the Spirit. We have not learned how to deal with self; we distrust it, perhaps deny it, but we cannot forget it. We never quite get free from the ghost of self. It's not the pride of the flesh that hinders us, but the fear of that pride. We are embarrassed at praise or promotion and go about our work ill at ease, glancing over our shoulder, fearful that the ghost will appear to point a skinny finger at our pride.

So loud has been the pulpit denunciation of the flesh that we have gotten into a semipathological condition over it. We are suffering from a kind of flesh-shock which inhibits free activity. Fear lies upon us, a dry terror that chills to the bone. We are afraid of ourselves, of people, and of circumstances. Not daring to fight with carnal weapons and not knowing how to fight with spiritual ones, we cease to fight altogether and lie whimpering in our prayer chamber, consecrated but helpless.

Whether we like to admit it or not, this fear is stopping us. It is paralyzing our activities and destroying leadership among us. Satan is using a legitimate truth to make us darkly suspicious of our every effort and to confuse us in our labors for the Lord. Satan has turned the doctrine of human depravity into effective propaganda that has infected us with a mass-inferiority complex. Our leaders are afraid to lead because they cannot disso-

SATAN IS USING A LEGITIMATE TRUTH TO MAKE US DARKLY SUSPICIOUS OF OUR EVERY EFFORT AND TO CONFUSE US IN OUR LABORS FOR THE LORD.

ciate leadership from pride. Rightly refusing to do anything in their own name, they yet cannot get free to do much in the name of the Lord.

And the sad thing is that the false cults are taking advantage of our weakness. Undeterred by any inhibitions, they go on with amazing brass to spread their evil doctrines.

THE DEEPER LIFE IS NOT FEARFUL

We greatly need spiritual leaders, but we are turning out of our churches and schools young people who are, with few exceptions, wholly unfit for leadership. We habitually beat them down till we have shattered their confidence, and then, under the mistaken impression that shattered confidence is humility, we send them out in subconscious defeat, filled with unrecognized fear and haunted with the ghost of self. Such leaders soon find their place—the only place they are psychologically suited—and settle down into a little corner to minister to a restricted few week after tedious week while the challenge of the greater need goes unregarded. This tragic waste of manpower goes on year after year among us, and instead of being recognized for what it is, and corrected, it is justified, even lauded as a beautiful demonstration of Christlike humility.

The problem is a vital one and, we admit, easier to argue than to solve, because the solution will involve tears and anguish of heart. It will involve admission of error and a drastic revision of some of our cherished theories of the deeper life. Yet we must do something about it. Our future growth and prosperity depend upon it. We must discover a New Testament technique whereby we can destroy self-confidence without at the same time destroying confidence. We must teach our people that the Holy Ghost is not given us for our enjoyment, but to empower us for fearless adventuring in the name of our risen Lord. We must, by prayer and intellectual courage, break the stalemate. We must escape from that do-nothing pietism which has turned our impulses inward instead of outward, and we must stress the self-forgetting objectivity of true spirituality. Then we will move on toward the good land where we can begin and continue to work in the unhindered power of the Holy Ghost.

THE DEEPER LIFE IS MORE THAN INTELLECTUAL KNOWLEDGE

"It is one thing," said Henry Suso, "to hear for oneself a sweet lute, sweetly played, and quite another thing merely to hear about it."

And it is one thing, we may add, to hear truth inwardly for one's very self, and quite another thing merely to hear *about* it.

We do not wish to reflect on the genuineness of any man's religious experience; rather we rejoice in every small shred of true godliness that may yet remain among us in these days of superficiality and pretense. But an examination of the state of things in gospel churches creates a strong suspicion that an alarmingly high percentage of professing Christians today have never heard the lute for themselves. They have only been told about it by others. Their acquaintance with saving truth is by hearsay merely.

The mysterious Voice has never penetrated to their own inner ear.

Particularly is this true of the so-called deeper life. Even in those circles where the doctrines of the Spirit-filled life are taken for granted, there is a strange lack of inner certainty. We hear the "deeper" truths recited with a glibness that makes us wonder whether the preacher is not telling us about something of which he has only heard, rather than about something which he himself has experienced. The widespread indoctrination in the deeper life without a corresponding enjoyment of the power of the doctrine may easily do more harm than good.

We are turning out from the Bible schools of this country year after year young men and women who know the theory of the Spirit-filled life but do not enjoy the experience. These go out into the churches to create in turn a generation of Christians who have never felt the power of the Spirit and who know nothing personally about the inner fire. The next generation will drop even the theory. That is actually the course some holiness groups have taken over the past years.

One word from the lips of the man who has actually heard the lute play will have more effect than a score of sermons by the man who has only heard that it was played. Acquaintance is always better than hearsay.

How long must we in America go on listening to men who can only tell us what they have read and heard about, never what they themselves have felt and heard and seen?

5

A STRONG DESIRE FOR GOD

*We get what we want, so our spiritual condition
perfectly corresponds to the intensity of our desire.
When you change these desires, the person of Christ
will become dear beyond expression.*

In my exploration on the deeper life, I am not referring to the starting point, the essence of personal salvation. The doctrines of blood atonement, of grace, of justification by faith apart from works—these are not before us. It is assumed that my readers hold to these precious and indispensable truths, and that they have each one personally trusted Christ for forgiveness of sin and life eternal. We are here occupied with the problem of the subsequent life, the life in the Spirit, with deliverance from the dead weight of our old natures, and moral power to live as becometh saints.

Since all true Christians have started out as equals, have drunk from the same fountain, have been washed in the same blood and renewed by the same Spirit, why do they differ so widely in the purity and power of their subsequent spiritual lives? For it cannot be denied that as "one star differeth from another star in glory," and one saint differeth from another saint in the resurrection, so do the saints differ from one another in the degree of their spiritual perfection right here in this present world.

GOD'S PLAN FOR ALL CHRISTIANS

Now it is most important that we locate the source of this difference, where it is, and not where it is not. We must not, for instance, assume that God in His sovereign pleasure has decreed that one of His children should be dull and earthly in spiritual tone and another radiant with the grace and power of the Spirit.

Christians differ from each other in gifts and abilities (and this by the will of God); but where their differences are of a spiritual nature and have to do with power and worship and inward radiance, the explanation is to be found elsewhere than in the will of God. "The fault, dear Brutus, is not in our stars, but in ourselves, that we are underlings." And the fault, dear Christian, is not in the will of God, but in ourselves, that we are weaklings. God wills that we should all be "filled with the fullness of God"; He desires that we should walk in the Spirit and know in actual experience that "great grace" which was upon the first Christians, and is upon a rare one here and there even in our day.

We must not draw back from the light, even when it reveals some things in our lives deeply humiliating to us. We shall be far wiser if we do as Ezekiel did: eat the roll no matter what the consequence may be. The habit of always looking for comfort in the Scriptures is not a commendable one. The truth is that we sometimes need other things much more critically than comfort. Now let us ask ourselves some uncomfortable questions.

WHAT WENT WRONG?

Why is it that there is in our fundamental churches so much light and so little delight? For no one can deny that we have much light. A world of annotated Bibles, commentaries, spiritual books, and sound magazines is all about us. Bible schools, excellent Christian colleges, sound preachers of the Word—these are with us in greater numbers than ever before. And yet the prevailing emotional tone among Christians these days is definitely not one of spiritual delight.

We present a pretty glum aspect for the most part, and our religious gatherings have need of artificial stimulation to generate enough synthetic joy to save us from outright gloom. Rarely do we see evidence of such supernatural radiance as is noted in the records of the early church, or found among the Moravians and Methodists of more recent times.

Why does so much truth result in so little fruit? Why does the average Christian read the Word so much with so little resulting that is supernatural and heavenly? Why do we buy so many splendid books on Bible truth and find them disappointing? Why do we pray so often and at such length with so little good coming of it? Why are we Christians so much like other people, when we should be ablaze with the light of God's face? Why do

WE PRESENT A PRETTY GLUM ASPECT FOR THE MOST PART, AND OUR RELIGIOUS GATHERINGS HAVE NEED OF ARTIFICIAL STIMULATION TO GENERATE ENOUGH SYNTHETIC JOY TO SAVE US FROM OUTRIGHT GLOOM.

we so seldom see the King in His beauty or have glimpses of that land which is very far off?

I think I know the answer to all these questions. Here it is. *Our trouble is lack of strong desire.*

Strong desire is indispensable to progress in godliness, yet it is just what is missing from the church of our day. With our fear of religious works—a kind of hallmark of orthodoxy—a longing after God is taken as evidence that we do not understand what the Bible teaches about grace.

But that is exactly contrary to the fact. Moses, who found grace in God's sight, used the fact as an argument for receiving more grace. "Now therefore, I pray thee, if I have found grace in thy sight, shew me now thy way, that I may know thee, that I may find grace in thy sight: and consider that this nation is thy people" (Ex. 33:13). Grace unto grace is the traditional formula of the thirsty saints, never grace unto complacency.

David was another believing man who never reached the place where he would say "enough" in his desire after God. His longing was so mighty that we in these lukewarm times can hardly stand before the heat of it. He longed for God with a desire so acute that it affected him physically. "O God, thou art my God; early will I seek thee: my soul thirsteth for thee, my flesh longeth for thee in a dry and thirsty land, where no water is; to see thy power and thy glory, so as I have seen thee in the sanctuary" (Ps. 63:1, 2).

Whatever timid expositors may do with these verses, there are some who know by personal experience how David felt. A brother minister, the pastor of one of Chicago's Bible churches, told me recently that his thirst for God had become so acute that it was affecting his physical body. He could literally feel in his mortal flesh the strivings of his soul after God.

Let no one stand aloof from such witness. A longing like that is not remotely akin to fanaticism, but has been one of the most conspicuous marks of spiritual greatness. The absence of it constitutes one of the heaviest problems in the church today.

In Jerusalem, sometime after Pentecost, a situation arose which required the appointment of seven young men to the work of serving tables in the community of the Christians. Their names are recorded in Acts 6 for us: Stephen, Philip, Prochorus, Nicanor, Timon, Parmenas, and Nicolas.

These men no doubt carried on their work faithfully, Stephen included. But while Stephen's hands held the tray, his soul was leaping up after all the spiritual riches his being could contain. And God was not slow to respond. "And Stephen, full of faith and power, did great wonders and miracles among the people" (Acts 6:8). They who disputed with him soon found that they "were not able to resist the wisdom and the spirit by which he spake" (v. 10). When he was finally called before the council, they "saw his face as it had been the face of an angel" (v. 15).

Philip, another of the seven, also left tables to become an evangelist; but he never rose to the daring heights of the man Stephen. Only the face of Stephen was as the face of an angel.

Every pastor who has had experience watching over the flock of God knows why Stephen went on to surpass the others. Briefly stated it was simply this: Stephen had a more intense desire after God and spiritual things. He blazed upward after God like the bush that burned, and his soul found Him after whom he so ardently longed.

It is not an uncommon sight in any church to see one or two in the congregation who are ablaze for God, while the rest accept things rather calmly and without much interest. They are saved, to be sure, and they are certain of their position before God; but farther than that their desire just does not lead them. If they grow at all, it is in doctrinal knowledge, not in spiritual fervor. They are content to know from the Scriptures that they have eternal life.

Many of them will engage in the routine service of teaching in the Sunday school, singing in the choir, passing out tracts, making a neighborhood canvass; but the eager pastor does not see among them anything resembling the face of an angel. Their spiritual awareness does not become acute; their love for the Triune God never gets out of hand, never causes them to thirst and long for God till their flesh suffers under the struggle.

More than a quarter of a century of pastoral work has taught me that most Christians simply will not cultivate their souls. They will not discipline their lives to bring them under the control of the Spirit. They will not die to self. They will not make the knowledge of God the single passion of their days and years. A few will and do, and they are the salt and seed of the truth in every generation.

THEIR LOVE FOR THE TRIUNE GOD NEVER GETS OUT OF HAND, NEVER CAUSES THEM TO THIRST AND LONG FOR GOD TILL THEIR FLESH SUFFERS UNDER THE STRUGGLE.

PAUL'S VEHEMENT DESIRE

Paul once used the significant phrase *vehement desire*, and though he did not apply it to himself, he could hardly have found a more accurate phrase to describe his own spiritual life. He burned with desire to know Christ, to experience for himself the "excellency of the knowledge of Christ Jesus my Lord" (Phil. 3:8). This holy vehemence carried him onward like a torrent to the end of his days.

Spiritual vehemence frightens the timid saints, but it carries the bolder ones upward to blessed spiritual heights. I wonder whether any great work has ever sprung up in any place apart from the presence of a few who were ablaze with vehement desire.

A classic example of the power of holy desire is found in the person of Evan Roberts, who was the human agent in the Welsh revival. His testimony is most revealing and can be downright startling unless we have some measure of the same spirit to prepare us for the shock.

The language he uses to describe his experiences furnishes a splendid expression of that spiritual vehemence of which I speak.

Suddenly I was wakened up out of my sleep, and I found myself, with unspeakable joy and awe, in the very presence of Almighty God. And for the space of four hours I was privileged to speak face to face with Him, as a man speaks to his friend. At four o'clock it seemed to me that I again returned to earth. . . .

Shortly some wonderful influence came over me. I felt some living energy of force entering my bosom. It held my breath. My legs trembled terribly. This living energy increased as one after the other prayed, until it nearly burst me. . . . My bosom boiled all through, and if I had not prayed I would have burst. What boiled my bosom? It was the verse, 'For God commendeth his love.' I fell on my knees with my arms stretched out on the seat before me. The perspiration poured down my face. And my tears streamed so quickly I thought the blood came out. It was awful on me for about ten minutes. I cried, 'Bend me, bend me, Oh! Oh! Oh!' . . . After I was bent a wave of peace filled my soul.

For a full generation in this country some of our leading Bible expositors have spent their time proving to us that there is no need for such spiritual vehemence as this, and during that time we have grown progressively colder until today the whole idea of personal saintliness has been all but lost to us. Thus the conditions around us successfully refute the objectors.

WE GET WHAT WE WANT

It may be set down as an axiom that our spiritual state perfectly corresponds to the intensity of our desire. Each of us enjoys as much grace as he actually wants. Where there seems to be a discrepancy between what we possess and what we desire to possess, we may safely conclude that our desire is not as great as we had supposed. We want God, it is true, *but we want something else more.* And we get what we want most.

What shall we do when we find that our desire is but lukewarm? Treat our condition as a spiritual sickness and act accordingly. Go to God about it as we would about any other sin, and stay before Him in penitence and faith till the flame of pure desire begins to glow within.

With the coming of strong desire a whole new world will open before us. The simplest Bible truth will come alive with a new and blessed meaning. The person of Christ will become dear beyond expression, and our lives will begin to glow with a fresh and wonderful devotion.

WHAT SHALL WE DO WHEN WE FIND THAT OUR DESIRE IS BUT LUKEWARM? TREAT OUR CONDITION AS A SPIRITUAL SICKNESS AND ACT ACCORDINGLY.

6

SPIRITUAL AMBITION

Spiritual change comes from the power of the Word and the power of the Spirit, but must be accompanied by our own efforts. Be aggressive! Claim the grace of God that He has given us as you move toward maturity.

If, as I firmly believe, every Christian possesses the keys to a life of spiritual power and personal communion with God, the seeker for such life faces an obvious and important question. How can such a plane be reached? How may we enter in and claim this land of spiritual promise?

I suggest first that we rouse ourselves from our state of religious passivity and develop a lot of tough aggressiveness. Something of Jacob's "I-will-not-let-thee-go" spirit is what we need very badly.

In view of the example of the great worshipers in Bible times and since, it is hard to understand the popularity of the philosophy of spiritual passivity which has laid hold of so many gospel

Christians today, with such unfortunate results. Even a scanty acquaintance with the lives of the spiritually great will show us how far from the truth such a philosophy really is.

The mighty among Old Testament believers were always those who were haunted by a deep discontent, a yearning after God which knew no limit nor end. The Bible saints were almost every one ridden with this holy inward burden. Deep dissatisfaction with their own progress, painful self-disapprobation, determination to know God more perfectly and intimately—these characteristics marked the great of the Bible.

And the saints of postbiblical times are not different. The record of their struggles is sometimes painful to read. An example in relatively recent times is David Brainerd, the American missionary to the Indians. His journal is replete with entries so full of self-condemnation, so plaintive in their cry after God and personal holiness as to fill us with sharpest pangs of sympathy as we read.

We rise from a perusal of his *Journal*, wondering whether this man was indeed a brother to the flock of contented sheep that fills the orthodox fold in our day. And we are troubled with the thought that there may have been some organic relationship between his spiritual anguish and that power which forced the Indians to their knees as he preached. Have we discovered an easier way to power, or have we simply learned to be content without it?

If we would go forward in the spiritual life, we must become aggressive in our determination and our faith. We must set advanced goals before us and drive toward them. "This one thing I do" must motivate our activities. We must also locate a number of closer objectives and go after them one at a time, taking each near position sharply and cleanly before moving on to the next.

This is to be sharply distinguished from that mere multiplying of religious chores which is some people's idea of a fuller Christian life. Indeed, it may even be desirable to call a moratorium on all so-called service till we have gotten acquainted with God and our own souls. "Be still and know" may easily be the most appropriate text for us right now, conditions being what they are.

VIGOROUS REJECTING

Before we can know God in growing intimacy it will be necessary that we do some vigorous rejecting. We shall need to reject everything that hinders our progress. We shall need to reject the sin that doth so easily beset us, the world in all its subtle forms, and every claim of the flesh to indulgence, however refined and pleasurable it may seem to be. We shall need to deny our ego and repudiate every carnal ambition.

Though it may seem to be a "hard saying," it must nevertheless be said: we must recognize and reject every form of pseudo-Christianity which may present itself to us under the cloak of orthodoxy. There is much of this, and it dare not be charitably excused or weakly tolerated.

Such variants of true Christianity may be identified in our day by the soundness of their doctrine and the unsoundness of their manners and morals. They are promoted by cheap methods; their spirit and mood are those of the radio skit; they embody in their "soul-winning" efforts the general tastes of the beauty contest and offer the prize of fleshly amusement to those who march in their gaudy parade. Their worship is alive with shiny superficialities, clever quips and bright small talk about Jesus.

The seeker after God will think of such in love, and his prayer will be, "Father, forgive them, for they know not what they do." But from such he will turn away.

It is difficult to aspire to better things without unintentionally reflecting upon those who are satisfied with something less, and it is difficult to gain loftier heights without looking down upon those who mill around in the shadows below. Such is one of the hazards of the spiritual life. The timid may avoid this temptation by sitting down with the rest and letting his spiritual ambition die. The courageous will press on and trust by humility and true penitence to keep his heart lowly and full of charity.

RESOLUTIONS FOR SPIRITUAL CHANGE

The aggressive seeker after God will need to make and keep certain resolutions. He will vow to honor God in every moment of his life and to accept any honor that may come to him as actually belonging to God. He must determine to surrender everything to God, to permit himself to be treated unjustly by others, to see other persons pushed to the front, to be treated with contempt by the popular leaders of the religious world and looked upon as something of a relic from another and quainter age. And all this he must accept without resentment or inward irritation.

As we go on toward our spiritual goal, several changes will be noted in our inward lives. We shall experience a wondrous sense of light, especially light upon the Scriptures. The Bible will begin to reach our spirits, deeper down and further in than that area usually affected by doctrinal instruction. The truth will be the same, but we shall be getting the living essence now instead of the mere letter.

Another change will be the coming of a purer and more heavenly mood as a fairly constant spiritual state. Our taste for the lighter religious songs will be lost and the real meaning of the great hymns will come upon us like waves of delight.

For the cultivation of the spiritual life, I recommend an acquaintance with the devotional classics which have meant so much to Christians of past ages. They are definitely to be chosen over the latest output of the religious press or the book written last week or last month.

Then there is that great wealth of devotional poetry which awaits discovery and which will reward us with a new and tender appreciation of divine things. We may well ignore the endless effusions of fifth-rate verse turned out by the yard by uninspired persons who go on rhyming "grace" with "face" and "in" with "sin" for tedious pages. The poetry of Isaac Watts, Charles Wesley, Frederick Faber, and St. Bernard, to name a few, will be like wells of refreshing water to the thirsty soul.

The sermons of certain mighty preachers of the past who lived in dark times will also help to sharpen our zest for the things of God; Tauler and Eckhart, for example. The devotional writings of such men as Fénelon, Law, Andrews, and Thomas à Kempis will prove of great help in our search for a better Christian life.

All this we must do with intelligence and determination, remembering always to trust the Word and the Spirit to lead us on.

If such advice as I have given here seems too dull or too impractical for these times, then we may as well resign ourselves to further wandering in the wilderness, for it is pretty evident that

that brand of nervous and shallow Christianity so popular today will never bring us into the promised land.

But let us rise up and pursue our way, humbly making use of such means of grace as God has put at our disposal and keeping our hearts open to hear His voice, even when it comes to us from an unfamiliar direction. The land is before us. Let us dare to enter in.

7

GIFTS OF THE SPIRIT

The apostle Paul urges us to "covet" and "desire"
spiritual gifts, but many of us have little understanding
about them. Your life and your churches can be transformed
by recognizing this power for service.

Concerning spiritual gifts, brethren," wrote Paul to the Corinthians, "I would not have you ignorant" (1 Cor. 12:1).

Certainly Paul meant nothing derogatory by this. Rather, he was expressing a charitable concern that his fellow believers should be neither uninformed nor in error about a truth so very important as this one.

For some time it has been evident that we evangelicals have been failing to avail ourselves of the deeper riches of grace that lie in the purposes of God for us. As a consequence, we have been suffering greatly, even tragically. One blessed treasure we have missed is the right to possess the gifts of the Spirit as set forth in such fullness and clarity in the New Testament.

Before proceeding further, however, I want to make it plain that I have had no change of mind about the matter. What I write here has been my faith for many years. No recent spiritual experience has altered my beliefs in any way. I merely bring together truths which I have held during my entire public ministry and have preached with a fair degree of consistency where and when I felt my hearers could receive them.

In their attitude toward the gifts of the Spirit, Christians over the last few years have tended to divide themselves into three groups.

First, there are those who magnify the gifts of the Spirit until they can see little else.

Second, there are those who deny that the gifts of the Spirit are intended for the church in this period of her history.

Third, there are those who appear to be thoroughly bored with the whole thing and do not care to discuss it.

More recently we have become aware of another group, so few in number as scarcely to call for classification. It consists of those who want to know the truth about the Spirit's gifts and to experience whatever God has for them within the context of sound New Testament faith. This is written for these few—those who want to learn about the gifts.

THE TRUE CHURCH

Every spiritual problem is at bottom theological. Its solution will depend upon the teaching of the Holy Scriptures plus a correct understanding of that teaching. That correct understanding constitutes a spiritual philosophy, that is, a viewpoint, a high vantage ground from which the whole landscape may be seen at once, each detail appearing in its proper relation to everything else. Once such vantage ground is gained, we are in a position to evaluate any teaching or interpretation that is offered us in the name of truth.

A proper understanding of the gifts of the Spirit in the church must depend upon a right concept of the nature of the church. The gift problem cannot be isolated from the larger question and settled by itself.

The true church is a spiritual phenomenon appearing in human society and intermingling with it to some degree but differing from it sharply in certain vital characteristics. It is composed of regenerated persons who differ from other human beings in that they have a superior kind of life imparted to them at the time of their inward renewal.

They are children of God in a sense not true of any other created beings.

Their origin is divine and their citizenship is in heaven.

They worship God in the Spirit, rejoice in Jesus Christ and have no confidence in the flesh.

They constitute a chosen generation, a royal priesthood, a holy nation, a peculiar people.

They have espoused the cause of a rejected and crucified Man who claimed to be God and who has pledged His sacred honor that He will prepare a place for them in His Father's house and return again to conduct them there with rejoicing.

In the meantime, they carry His cross, suffer whatever indignities men may heap upon them for His sake, act as His ambassadors, and do good to all men in His name.

They steadfastly believe that they will share His triumph, and for this reason they are perfectly willing to share His rejection by a society that does not understand them.

And they have no hard feelings—only charity and compassion and a strong desire that all men may come to repentance and be reconciled to God.

This is a fair summary of one aspect of New Testament teaching about the church. But another truth more revealing and significant to those seeking information about the gifts of the Spirit is that the church is a spiritual body, an organic entity united by the life that dwells within it.

EACH MEMBER JOINED TOGETHER

Each member is joined to the whole by a relationship of life. As a man's soul may be said to be the life of his body, so the indwelling Spirit is the life of the church.

The idea that the church is the body of Christ is not an erroneous one, resulting from the pressing too far of a mere figure of speech. The apostle Paul in three of his epistles sets forth this truth in such sobriety of tone and fullness of detail as to preclude the notion that he is employing a casual figure of speech not intended to be taken too literally. The clear, emphatic teaching of the great apostle is that Christ is the Head of the church which is His body. The parallel is drawn carefully and continued through long passages. Conclusions are drawn from the doctrine, and certain moral conduct is made to depend upon it.

As a normal man consists of a body with various obedient members and a head to direct them, so the true church is a body—

individual Christians being the members and Christ the Head.

The mind works through the members of the body, using them to fulfill its intelligent purposes. Paul speaks of the foot, the hand, the ear, the eye as being members of the body, each with its proper but limited function; but it is the Spirit that worketh in them (1 Cor. 12:1–31).

The teaching that the church is the body of Christ in 1 Corinthians 12 follows a listing of certain spiritual gifts and reveals the necessity for those gifts.

The intelligent head can work only as it has at its command organs designed for various tasks. It is the mind that sees, but it must have an eye to see through. It is the mind that hears, but it cannot hear without an ear.

And so with all the varied members which are the instruments by means of which the mind moves into the external world to carry out its plans.

As human work is done by our minds, so the work of the church is done by the Spirit, and by Him alone. But to work He must set in the body certain members with abilities specifically created to act as media through which the Spirit can flow toward ordained ends. That in brief is the philosophy of the gifts of the Spirit.

HOW MANY GIFTS?

It is often said that there are nine gifts of the Spirit. (I suppose because Paul lists nine in 1 Corinthians 12.) Actually, Paul mentions no less than seventeen (1 Cor. 12:4–11, 27–31; Rom. 12:3–8; Eph. 4:7–11). And these are not natural talents merely, but gifts imparted by the Holy Spirit to fit the believer for his place in the body of Christ. They are like pipes on a great organ, permitting the musician wide scope and range to produce music of the finest quality. But they are, I repeat, more than talents. They are spiritual gifts.

Natural talents enable a man to work within the field of nature; but through the body of Christ God is doing an eternal work above and beyond the realm of fallen nature. This requires supernatural working.

Religious work can be done by natural men without the gifts of the Spirit, and it can be done well and skillfully. But work designed for eternity can only be done by the eternal Spirit. No work has eternity in it unless it is done by the Spirit through gifts He has Himself implanted in the souls of redeemed men.

STILL FOR TODAY?

For a generation, certain evangelical teachers have told us that all the gifts of the Spirit ceased at the death of the apostles or at the completion of the New Testament. This, of course, is a doctrine without a syllable of biblical authority behind it. Its advocates must accept full responsibility for thus manipulating the Word of God.

The result of this erroneous teaching is that spiritually gifted persons are ominously few among us. When we so desperately need leaders with the gift of discernment, for instance, we do not have them and are compelled to fall back upon the techniques of the world.

This frightening hour calls aloud for men with the gift of prophetic insight. Instead we have men who conduct surveys, polls, and panel discussions.

Thus we may be preparing ourselves for the tragic hour when God may set us aside as so-called evangelicals and raise up another movement to keep New Testament Christianity alive on the earth. Say not, *we be children of Abraham*, and "God is able of these stones to raise up children unto Abraham" (Matt. 3:9).

The truth of the matter is that the Scriptures plainly imply the imperative of possessing the gifts of the Spirit. Paul urges that we both "covet" and "desire" spiritual gifts (1 Cor. 12:31; 14:1). It does not appear to be an optional matter with us but rather a scriptural mandate to those who have been filled with the Spirit.

EQUALLY VALUABLE?

I must also add a word of caution. The various spiritual gifts are not equally valuable, as Paul so carefully explained.

Certain brethren have magnified one of the seventeen gifts out of all proportion. Among these brethren there have been and are many godly souls, but the general moral results of this teaching have nevertheless not been good.

In practice it has resulted in much shameless exhibitionism, a tendency to depend upon experiences instead of upon Christ, and often a lack of ability to distinguish the works of the flesh from the operations of the Spirit.

Those who deny that the gifts are for us today and those who insist upon making a hobby of one gift are both wrong, and we are all suffering the consequence of their error.

Today there is no reason for our remaining longer in doubt. We have every right to expect our Lord to grant to His church the spiritual gifts which He has never in fact taken away from us, but which we are failing to receive only because of our error or unbelief.

It is more than possible that God is even now imparting the gifts of the Spirit to whomsoever He can and in whatever measure He can as His conditions are met, even imperfectly. Otherwise the torch of truth would flicker out and die. Clearly, however, we have yet to see what God would do for His church if we would all throw ourselves down before Him with an open Bible and cry, "Behold the handmaid of the Lord; be it unto me according to thy word" (Luke 1:38).

8

HOW TO BE FILLED WITH THE HOLY SPIRIT

With all of the confusing and contradictory teaching on the Holy Spirit, some people instinctively recoil at any mention of the Spirit's filling. Learn four simple words that point to a spiritual breakthrough.

Almost all Christians want to be *full* of the Spirit. Only a few want to be filled with the Spirit. But how can a Christian know the fullness of the Spirit unless he has known the experience of being filled?

It would, however, be useless to tell anyone how to be filled with the Spirit unless he first believes that he can be. No one can hope for something he is not convinced is the will of God for him and within the bounds of scriptural provision.

Before the question "How can I be filled?" has any validity, the seeker after God *must be sure that the experience of being filled is actually possible.* The man who is not sure can have no ground of expectation. Where there is no expectation there can be no faith, and where there is no faith the inquiry is meaningless.

The doctrine of the Spirit as it relates to the believer has been shrouded over the last half century in a mist such as lies upon a mountain in stormy weather. A world of confusion has surrounded this truth. The children of God have been taught contrary doctrines from the same texts, warned, threatened, and intimidated until they instinctively recoil from every mention of the Bible teaching concerning the Holy Spirit.

This confusion has not come by accident. An enemy has done this. Satan knows that Spiritless evangelicalism is as deadly as modernism or heresy, and he has done everything in his power to prevent us from enjoying our true Christian heritage.

A church without the Spirit is as helpless as Israel might have been in the wilderness if the fiery cloud had deserted them. The Holy Spirit is our cloud by day and our fire by night. Without Him we only wander aimlessly about the desert.

That is what we today are surely doing. We have divided ourselves into little ragged groups, each one running after a will-o'-the-wisp or firefly in the mistaken notion that we are following the Shekinah glory. It is not only desirable that the cloudy pillar should begin to glow again. It is imperative.

BELIEVE IN THE SPIRIT'S FILLING

The church can have light only as it is full of the Spirit, and it can be full only as the members that compose it are filled individually. Furthermore, no one can be filled until he is convinced that being filled is a part of the total plan of God in redemption; that it is nothing added or extra, nothing strange or unusual, but a proper and spiritual operation of God, based upon and growing out of the work of Christ in atonement.

The inquirer must be sure to the point of conviction. He must believe that the whole thing is normal and right. He must believe that God wills that he be anointed with a horn of fresh oil beyond and in addition to all the ten thousand blessings he may already have received from the good hand of God.

Until he is so convinced I recommend that he take time out to fast and pray and meditate upon the Scriptures. Faith comes from the Word of God. Suggestion, exhortation, or the psychological effect of the testimony of others who may have been filled will not suffice.

Unless he is persuaded from the Scriptures he should not press the matter nor allow himself to fall victim to the emotional manipulators intent upon forcing the issue. God is wonderfully patient and understanding and will wait for the slow heart to catch up with the truth. In the meantime, the seeker should be calm and confident. In due time God will lead him through the Jordan. Let him not break loose and run ahead. Too many have done so, only to bring disaster upon their Christian lives.

DESIRE THE SPIRIT'S FILLING

After a man is convinced that he can be filled with the Spirit, he *must desire to be.* To the interested inquirer I ask these questions: Are you sure that you want to be possessed by a Spirit who, while He is pure and gentle and wise and loving, will yet insist upon being Lord of your life? Are you sure you want your personality to be taken over by One who will require obedience to the written Word? Who will not tolerate any of the self-sins in your life, such as self-love and self-indulgence? Who will not permit you to strut or boast or show off? Who will take the direction of your life away from you and will reserve the sovereign right to test you and discipline you? Who will strip away from you many loved objects which secretly harm your soul?

Unless you can answer an eager "Yes" to these questions, you do not want to be filled. You may want the thrill or the victory or the power, but you do not really want to be filled with the Spirit. Your desire is little more than a feeble wish and is not pure enough to please God, who demands all or nothing.

Again I ask: Are you sure you *need to be filled* with the Spirit? Tens of thousands of Christians, laymen, preachers, and missionaries manage to get on somehow without having had a clear experience of being filled. That Spiritless labor can lead only to tragedy in the day of Christ is something the average Christian seems to have forgotten. But how about you?

Perhaps your doctrinal bias is away from belief in the crisis of the Spirit's filling. Very well, look at the fruit of such doctrine. What is your life producing? You are doing religious work, preaching, singing, writing, promoting, but what is the *quality* of your work? True, you received the Spirit at the moment of conversion, but is it also true that you are ready without a further anointing to resist temptation, obey the Scriptures, understand the truth, live victoriously, die in peace, and meet Christ without embarrassment at His coming?

If, on the other hand, your soul cries out for God, for the living God, and your dry and empty heart despairs of living a normal Christian life without a further anointing, then I ask you: Is your desire all-absorbing? Is it the biggest thing in your life? Does it crowd out every common religious activity and fill you with an acute longing that can only be described as the pain of desire? If your heart cries "Yes" to these questions you may be on your way to a spiritual breakthrough that will transform your whole life.

> **WHAT IS YOUR LIFE PRODUCING? YOU ARE DOING RELIGIOUS WORK, PREACHING, SINGING, WRITING, PROMOTING, BUT WHAT IS THE *QUALITY* OF YOUR WORK?**

PREPARE FOR THE SPIRIT'S FILLING

It is in the preparation for receiving the Spirit's anointing that most Christians fail. Probably no one was ever filled without first having gone through a period of deep soul disturbance and inward turmoil. When we find ourselves entering this state, the temptation is to panic and draw back. Satan exhorts us to take it easy lest we make shipwreck of the faith, and dishonor the Lord that bought us.

Of course Satan cares nothing for us nor for our Lord. His purpose is to keep us weak and unarmed in a day of conflict.

And millions of believers accept his hypocritical lies as gospel truth and go back to their caves like the prophets of Obadiah to feed on bread and water.

SATAN EXHORTS US TO TAKE IT EASY LEST WE MAKE SHIPWRECK OF THE FAITH, AND DISHONOR THE LORD THAT BROUGHT US.

Before there can be fullness there must be emptiness. Before God can fill us with Himself we must first be emptied of ourselves. It is this emptying that brings the painful disappointment and despair of self of which so many persons have complained just prior to their new and radiant experience.

There must come a total of self-devaluation, a death to all things without us and within us, or there can never be a real filling with the Holy Spirit.

> *The dearest idol I have known,*
> *Whate'er that idol be,*
> *Help me to tear it from Thy throne,*
> *And worship only Thee.*

We sing this glibly enough, but we cancel out our prayer by our refusal to surrender the very idol of which we sing. To give up our last idol is to plunge ourselves into a state of inward loneliness which no gospel meeting, no fellowship with other Christians, can ever cure. For this reason most Christians play it safe and settle for a life of compromise.

They have some of God, to be sure, but not all; and God has some of them, but not all. And so they live their tepid lives and try to disguise with bright smiles and snappy choruses the deep spiritual destitution within them.

One thing should be made crystal clear: The soul's journey through the dark night is not a meritorious one. The suffering and the loneliness do not make a man dear to God nor earn the horn of oil for which he yearns. We cannot buy anything from God. Everything comes out of His goodness on the grounds of Christ's redeeming blood and is a free gift, with no strings attached.

The soul agony breaks up the fallow ground, empties the vessel, detaches the heart from earthly interests, and focuses the attention upon God.

FOUR SIMPLE WORDS

All that has gone before is by way of soul preparation for the divine act of infilling. The infilling itself is not a complicated thing. While I shy away from "how to" formulas in spiritual things, I believe the answer to the question "How can I be filled?" may be answered in four words, all of them active verbs: (1) *surrender*, (2) *ask*, (3) *obey*, and (4) *believe*.

Surrender: "I beseech you therefore, brethren, by the mercies of God, that ye present your bodies a living sacrifice, holy, acceptable unto God, which is your reasonable service. And be not conformed to this world: but be ye transformed by the renewing of your mind, that ye may prove what is that good, and acceptable, and perfect, will of God" (Rom. 12:1, 2).

Ask: "If ye then, being evil, know how to give good gifts unto your children: how much more shall your heavenly Father give the Holy Spirit to them that ask him?" (Luke 11:13).

Obey: "We are his witnesses of these things; and so is also the Holy Ghost, whom God hath given to them that obey him" (Acts 5:32).

Complete and ungrudging obedience to the will of God is absolutely indispensable to the reception of the Spirit's anointing. As we wait before God we should reverently search the Scriptures and listen for the voice of gentle stillness to learn what our heavenly Father expects of us. Then, trusting to His enabling, we should obey to the best of our ability and understanding.

Believe: "This only would I learn of you, Received ye the Spirit by the works of the law, or by the hearing of faith?" (Gal. 3:2).

While the infilling of the Spirit is received by faith and only by faith, let us beware of that imitation faith which is no more than a mental assent to truth. It has been a source of great disappointment to multitudes of seeking souls. True faith invariably brings a witness.

But what is that witness? It is nothing physical, vocal, or psychical. The Spirit never commits Himself to the flesh. The only witness He gives is a subjective one, known to the individual alone. The Spirit announces Himself to the deepest part of our spirit. The flesh profiteth nothing, but the believing heart knows (see John 6:63–69). *Holy, holy, holy.*

One last thing: Neither in the Old Testament nor in the New, nor in Christian testimony as found in the writings of the saints as far as my knowledge goes, was any believer ever filled with the Holy Spirit *who did not know he had been filled.* Neither was anyone filled *who did not know when he was filled.* And *no one was ever filled gradually.*

Behind these three trees many halfhearted souls have tried to hide like Adam from the presence of the Lord, but they are not good enough hiding places. The man who does not know when he was filled was never filled (though of course it is possible to forget the date). And the man who hopes to be filled gradually will never be filled at all.

In my sober judgment, the relation of the Spirit to the believer is the most vital question the church faces today. The problems raised by Christian existentialism or neoorthodoxy are nothing by comparison with this most critical one. Ecumenicity, eschatological theories—none of these things deserve consideration until every believer can give an affirmative answer to the question, "Have ye received the Holy Ghost since ye believed?" (Acts 19:2).

And it might easily be that after we have been filled with the Spirit we will find to our delight that the very filling itself has solved the other problems for us.

9

FIVE VOWS FOR SPIRITUAL POWER

There is strength in being bound—if the bonds are self-imposed so that God may have His way completely. Discover five practical applications of the deeper spiritual life.

Some people object to taking vows, but in the Bible you will find many great men of God directed by covenants, promises, vows, and pledges. The psalmist was not averse to the taking of vows. "Thy vows are upon me, O God," he said. "I will render praises unto thee" (Ps. 56:12).

My counsel in this matter is that if you are really concerned about spiritual improvement—the gaining of new power, new life, new joy, and new personal revival within your heart—you will do well to make certain vows and proceed to keep them. If you should fail, go down in humility and repent and start over.

But always keep these vows before you. They will help harmonize your heart with the vast powers that flow out and down from the throne where Christ sitteth at the right hand of God.

A carnal man refuses the discipline of such commitments. He says, "I want to be free. I don't want to lay any vows upon myself; I don't believe in it. It is legalism." Well, let me paint a picture of two men.

One of them will not take vows. He will not accept any responsibility. He wants to be free. And he is free, in a measure—just as a vagrant is free. The vagrant is free to sit on a park bench by day, sleep on a newspaper by night, get chased out of town on Thursday morning, and find his way up a set of creaky stairs in some flophouse on Thursday night. Such a man is free, but he is also useless.

BUT THE GREAT SOULS ARE ONES WHO HAVE GONE REVERENTLY TO GOD WITH THE UNDERSTANDING THAT IN THEIR FLESH DWELLS NO GOOD THING.

Let's look at another man—maybe a president or prime minister or any great man who carries upon himself the weight of government. Such men are not free. But in the sacrifice of their freedom they step up their power. If they insist upon being free, they can be free, just like the vagrant. But they choose rather to be bound.

There are many religious vagrants in the world who will not be bound by anything. They have turned the grace of God into personal license. But the great souls are ones who have gone reverently to God with the understanding that in their flesh dwells no good thing. And they know that without God's enablement, any vows taken would be broken before sundown. Nevertheless, believing in God, reverently they took certain sacred vows. This is the way to spiritual power.

Now there are five vows I have in mind which we do well to make and keep.

VOW #1: DEAL THOROUGHLY WITH SIN

Sin has been driven underground these days and has come up with a new name and face. You may be subjected to this phenomenon in the schools. Sin is being called by various fancy names—anything but what it really is. For example, men don't get under conviction anymore; they get a guilt complex. Instead of confessing their guilt to God and getting rid of it, they lie on a couch and try to tell a man who ought to know better all about themselves. It comes out after a while that they were deeply disappointed when they were two years old or some such thing. That's supposed to make them better.

The whole thing is ridiculous, because sin is still the ancient enemy of the soul. It has never changed. We've got to deal firmly with sin in our lives. Let's remember that. "The kingdom of God is not meat and drink," said Paul, "but righteousness, and peace, and joy in the Holy Ghost" (Rom. 14:17). Righteousness lies at the door of the kingdom of God. "The soul that sinneth, it shall die" (Ezek. 18:4).

This is not to preach sinless perfection. This is to say that every known sin is to be named, identified, and repudiated, and that we must trust God for deliverance from it, so that there is no conscious, deliberate sin anywhere in our lives. It is absolutely necessary that we deal thus, because God is a holy God and sin is on the throne of the world.

So don't call your sins by some other name. If you're jealous, call it jealousy. If you tend to pity yourself and feel that you are not appreciated, but are like a flower born to blush unseen and waste your sweetness on the desert air, call it what it is—self-pity.

There is resentfulness. If you're resentful, admit it. I have met people who live in a state of sputtering indignation most of the time. I know of a preacher who acts like a hen thrown out of the nest. He keeps running in all directions clucking and complaining—somebody is always doing him wrong. Well, if you have got that spirit, you must deal with it now. You must get that out of you. The blood of Jesus Christ cleanses from all sin. Instead of covering it up and trying to find a Greek marginal rendering somewhere to hide it under, call it by its right name and get rid of it by the grace of God.

And then there is your temper. Don't call it indignation. Don't try to christen it by some other name. Call it what it is. Because if you have a bad temper you will either get rid of it or it will get rid of much of your spirituality and most of your joy.

So let's deal with sin thoroughly. Let's be perfectly candid. God loves candid people.

VOW #2: NEVER OWN ANYTHING

I do not mean by this that you cannot have things. I mean that you ought to get delivered from the sense of possessing them. This sense of possessing is what hinders us. All babies are born with their fists clenched, and it seems to me it means "This is mine!" One of the first things they say is "mine" in an angry voice. That sense of "This is mine" is a very injurious thing to the spirit. If you can get rid of it so that you have no feeling of possessing anything, there will come a great sense of freedom and liberty into your life.

Now don't think that you must sell all that you have and give it to charity. No. God will let you have your car and your business, your practice and your position, whatever it may be, provided you understand that it is not yours at all, but His, and all you are doing is just working for Him. You can be restful about it then, because we never need to worry about losing anything that belongs to someone else. If it is yours, you're always looking in your hand to see if it's still there. If it's God's, you no longer need to worry about it.

Let me point out some things you'll have to turn over to God. Property is one thing. Some of the dear Lord's children are being held back because there's a ball and chain on their legs. If it's a man, it's his big car and fine home. If it's a woman, it's her china and her Louis XIV furniture and all the rest. Take that vase for instance. There it stands, and if anybody knocked it off and broke it the poor owner would probably lose five years from her life!

VOW #3: NEVER DEFEND YOURSELF

We're all born with a desire to defend ourselves. And if you insist upon defending yourself, God will let you do it. But if you turn the defense of yourself over to God, He will defend you. He told Moses once, in Exodus 23: "I will be an enemy unto thine enemies, and an adversary unto thine adversaries" (v. 22).

IF YOU INSIST UPON DEFENDING YOURSELF, GOD WILL LET YOU DO IT. BUT IF YOU TURN THE DEFENSE OF YOURSELF OVER TO GOD, HE WILL DEFEND YOU.

A long time ago the Lord and I went through the twenty-third of Exodus together and He gave it to me. For thirty years now it has been a source of untold blessing to my life. I don't have to fight. The Lord does the fighting for me. And He'll do the same for you. He will be an enemy to your enemy and an adversary to your adversary, and you'll never need to defend yourself.

What do we defend? Well, we defend our talents, we defend our service, and particularly we defend our reputation. Your reputation is what people think you are, and if a story gets out about you, the big temptation is to try to run it down. But you know, running down the source of a story is a hopeless task. Absolutely hopeless! It's like trying to find the bird after you've found the feather on your lawn. You can't do it. But if you'll turn yourself wholly over to the Lord He will defend you completely and see to it that no one will harm you. "No weapon that is formed against thee shall prosper," He says, and "every tongue that shall rise against thee in judgment thou shalt condemn" (Isa. 54:17).

Henry Suso was a great Christian of other days. Once he was seeking what some Christians have told me they are seeking—to know God better. Let's put it like this: you are seeking to have a religious awakening within your spirit that will thrust you farther out into the deep things of God. Well, as Henry Suso was seeking God, people started telling evil stories about the man, and it grieved him so that he wept bitter tears and had great sorrow of heart.

Then one day he looked out the window and saw a dog playing on the lawn. The dog had a mat, and kept picking the mat up, tossing it over his shoulder, running and getting it, tossing it some more, picking it up and tossing it again. God said to Henry Suso, "That mat is your reputation, and I am letting the dogs of sin tear your reputation to shreds and toss it all over the lawn for your own good. One of these days things will change."

And things did change. It was not very long before the people who were tearing his reputation were confounded, and Suso rose into a place that made him a power in his day and a great blessing still to those who sing his hymns and read his works.

VOW #4: NEVER PASS ANYTHING ON ABOUT ANYBODY ELSE THAT WILL SLANDER HIM

"Charity shall cover the multitude of sins" (1 Peter 4:8). The talebearer has no place in God's favor. If you know something that would slander the reputation of one of God's children, bury it forever. Find a little garden out back—a little spot somewhere—and when somebody comes around with an evil story, take it out and bury it, and say, "Here lies in peace the story about my brother." God will take care of it. "With what judgment ye judge, ye shall be judged" (Matt. 7:2).

If you want God to be good to you, you are going to have to be good to His children. You say, "That's not grace." Well, grace gets you into the kingdom of God. That is unmerited favor. But after you are seated at the Father's table He expects to teach you table manners. And He won't let you eat unless you obey the etiquette of the table. And what is that? The etiquette of the table is that you don't tell stories about the brother who is sitting at the table with you—no matter what his denomination, or nationality, or background.

VOW #5: NEVER ACCEPT ANY GLORY

God is jealous of His glory and He will not give His glory to another. He will not even *share* His glory with another. It is quite natural, I should say, for people to hope that maybe their Christian service will give them a chance to display their talents. True, they want to serve the Lord. But they also want other people to know they are serving the Lord. They want to have a reputation among the saints. That is very dangerous ground—seeking a reputation among the saints. It's bad enough to seek a reputation in the world, but it's worse to seek a reputation among the people of God. Our Lord gave up His reputation, and so must we.

Meister Eckhart once preached a sermon on Christ cleansing the temple. He said, "Now there was nothing wrong with those men selling and buying there. There was nothing wrong with exchanging money there; it had to be. The sin lay in their doing it for profit. They got a percentage on serving the Lord." And then he made the application: "Anybody that serves for a commission—for what little bit of glory he can get out of it—is a merchant, and he ought to be cast out of the temple."

IT'S BAD ENOUGH TO SEEK A REPUTATION IN THE WORLD, BUT IT'S WORSE TO SEEK A REPUTATION AMONG THE PEOPLE OF GOD.

I go along with this. If you're serving the Lord, and yet slyly—perhaps scarcely known to you—you're hoping to get just a little 5 percent commission, then look out! It will chill the power of God in your spirit. You must determine that you will never take any glory, but see that God gets it all.

Now the easiest possible thing is to give a message like this. The hard thing is to make it work in one's own life. Remember that these five vows are not something you write in the back of your Bible and forget. They've got to be written in your own blood. They have to be made final, irrevocable. If it only comes off the surface, it's no good. Much of our consecration is just that way—it comes off the surface. Many of our promises come off the surface. No, no. Let it come out of the depths of your heart, the deep depths of your spirit.

These vows cut against the old human nature. They introduce the cross into your life. And nobody ever walks back from carrying his cross—nobody, ever. When a man takes his cross he's already said goodbye. He's pulled the roll top shut on his desk and said farewell to his wife and children. He's not coming back. The man with the cross never comes back. When you make these vows, remember: they introduce the cross into your life, they strike at the heart of your self-life, and there is never a place to go back to. And I say, "Woe to the triflers!"

In America—and maybe in other places too—so many people are saying, "Try Jesus, try God!" Triflers, experimenters, tasters they are. Like a rabbit with a half dozen holes so if one is stopped up he can flee to another! No! From the cross there is no place to flee. You don't "try" Jesus. He's not there to be experimented with. Christ is not on trial. You are. I am. He's not! God raised

Him from the dead and forever confirmed His deity and sealed Him and set Him at His own right hand as Lord and Christ. Turn everything over to Him and you'll find your life begin to lift. You'll blossom in a wonderful way.

Now, if you happen to be one of those on whom God has laid His hand for a deeper life, a more powerful life, a fuller life, then I wonder if you would be willing to pray this kind of prayer: "O God, glorify Thyself at my expense. Send me the bill—anything, Lord. I set no price. I will not dicker or bargain. Glorify Thyself. I'll take the consequences."

This kind of praying is simple, but it's deep and wonderful and powerful. I believe, if you can pray a prayer like that, it will be the ramp from which you can take off into higher heights and bluer skies in the things of the Spirit.

AS WE MOVE INTO DEEPER PERSONAL
ACQUAINTANCE WITH THE TRIUNE GOD I
THINK OUR LIFE EMPHASIS WILL SHIFT FROM
THE PAST AND THE PRESENT TO
THE FUTURE.

SLOWLY WE WILL BECOME CHILDREN OF
A LIVING HOPE AND SONS OF A SURE
TOMORROW. OUR HEARTS WILL BE TENDER
WITH MEMORIES OF YESTERDAY AND OUR
LIVES SWEET WITH GRATITUDE TO GOD FOR
THE SURE WAY WE HAVE COME; BUT OUR EYES
WILL BE FOCUSED MORE AND MORE UPON
THE BLESSED HOPE OF TOMORROW.

—A. W. TOZER

SOURCES

Chapter 1: "Are We Missing Something?" published as "Are We Fundamentalists Missing Something?" *Moody Monthly*, April 1950, 536. The first of three articles in a series commissioned to mark *Moody Monthly*'s fiftieth anniversary. The concluding section of the chapter was first published as "The Ministry of the Night," *Alliance Witness*, May 15, 1963, 2. Later published in *That Incredible Christian* (Chicago: Moody Publishers, 1964).

Chapter 2: "No Revival without Reformation," *Christian Life*, May 1957, 14–15.

Chapter 3: "The Deeper Life: What It Is," *Christian Life*, August 1957, 10–12, with additional material from "What Is the Deeper Life?," *Alliance Witness*, November 3, 1954, 2.

Chapter 4: "The Deeper Life: What It Is Not," compiled from three sources: Opening section of chapter from a sermon preached at Southside Alliance Church in Chicago, February 12, 1956, originally titled "Our Relationships to God" as the fourth of a four-sermon series; second section of chapter published as "Toward the Good Land: Breaking the Stalemate," *Alliance Witness*, August 30, 1941, 548–49; and "A Sweet Lute, Sweetly Played" (editorial), *Alliance Witness*, March 24, 1954, 2.

Chapter 5: "A Strong Desire for God," published as "The Vital Need for Strong Desire," *Moody Monthly*, May 1950, 659–60.

Chapter 6: "Spiritual Ambition," published as "The Place of Spiritual Aggressiveness," *Moody Monthly*, June 1950, 720–21.

Chapter 7: "Gifts of the Spirit," *Christian Life*, October 1957, 24–25.

Chapter 8: "How to Be Filled with the Holy Spirit," *Christian Life*, December 1957, 14–15.

Chapter 9: "Five Vows for Spiritual Power," *Moody Monthly*, September 1961, 22–23. After A. W. Tozer addressed the International Fellowship of Christian Students in 1961, Dr. William Culbertson heard a tape of the sermon and asked Tozer to edit it for *Moody Monthly* magazine.

Epilogue: "Praise in Three Dimensions," *Alliance Witness*, September 4, 1957, 2.

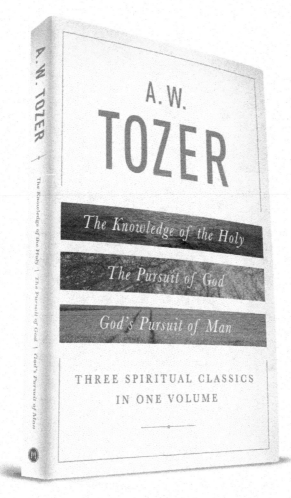

How do Christians grow?

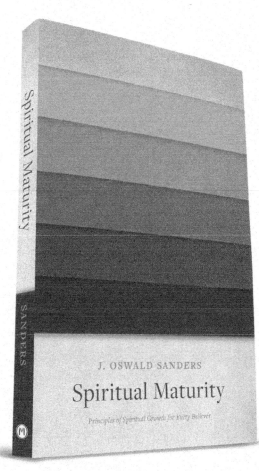

J. OSWALD SANDERS

Spiritual Maturity

Principles of Spiritual Growth for Every Believer